HEATHCLIFF

WANTED

by George Gately

C

CHARTER BOOKS, NEW YORK

HEATHCLIFF WANTED

A Charter Book / published by arrangement with
McNaught Syndicate, Inc.

PRINTING HISTORY
Seventeen Tempo printings
First Charter printing / December 1983
Third printing / January 1985

ISBN: 0-441-32211-5

WANTED:

Name: Heathcliff
Height: 13 inches
Weight: 12 pounds
Color: Orange
Distinguishing Characteristic: Able to create hilarity at the drop of a fishbowl.
Crimes: Fish robbery in the first degree
       Excessive garbage can dumping
       Impersonating a dog catcher
       Scratch post scuttling
       Bulldog baiting
       Milk truck marauding

Warning: This cat is armed with humor and may be dangerous to your funny bone.

"SAY!....YOU LOOK FAMILIAR!...."

© 1977
McNaught Synd., Inc.

"WHY CAN'T WE HAVE A DUMB OL' MASCOT
LIKE ANY OTHER TEAM ?!"

"ANYONE CARE FOR AN HORS D'OEUVRE?"

"THERE'S SOMEONE HERE TO SEE THE HEAD OF THE HOUSEHOLD!"

"CATS DON'T GET AN ALLOWANCE!"

"AWW!...DIDUMS FALL DOWN AND GO BOOM?!"

"PUT THAT BACK...WHERE YOU GOT IT!"

"YOUR CAT IS QUITE A RETRIEVER!"

"...AND HOW MUCH WOULD YOU CHARGE FOR THIS ENDORSEMENT?"

"HE NEVER ACCEPTS FOURTH RUNNER-UP!"

"THEY'D LIKE A SET OF MATCHED SCRATCHING POSTS."

"HEATHCLIFF HAS SET UP A KITTEN CROSSING!"

"I CAN'T FIND THE COOKING SHERRY!"

"YOU ARE ABOUT TO THRASH SOMEONE TO A PULP!"

"HOLD THE TUNA FISH!"

" STICK....

....'EM UP!"

"HE'S A VERY AGGRESSIVE MASCOT!"

"HE'S GOT A DUMPING PERMIT!"

"I SEE....AND WHERE ELSE DOES IT HURT?"

"HEAVENS!...I'LL BE GLAD WHEN WE GET OUR NEW PICTURE TUBE!"

"YOUR SON, HEATHCLIFF, IS HERE TO SEE YOU."

"I THOUGHT THIS CLUB HAD AN EXCLUSIVE MEMBERSHIP!"

© 1977
McNaught Synd., Inc.

"TONIGHT IT'S HIS BARBERSHOP QUARTET!"

"EVER GET THE FEELING SOMEONE IS PEERING OVER YOUR SHOULDER?!"

"HEATHCLIFF HAS DECIDED TO MAKE PEACE."

"DO YOU REALIZE HOW MANY CAT FIGHTS YOU'VE BEEN IN THIS WEEK ?!"

"NEVER MIND USING THE CALCULATOR !!"

"ANY OTHER COLLATERAL?"

2-12

"WE'RE MISSING A PENGUIN!"

"I'M OUT!"   "I FOLD!"   "I QUIT!"

" YOU HAVEN'T WON IT YET! "

© 1977
McNaught Synd., Inc.

2-19

TODAY
OUR
FOUR
FOOTED
FRIENDS

"I'M GLAD YOU ENJOYED THE SERMON."

"HEATHCLIFF HIRED A REFEREE."

"I'LL COMMENT ON THE REPORT CARD!"

"DOES HE ALWAYS INFLUENCE YOUR DECISIONS?"

"WOW!...WHAT HAPPENED TO YOU?!"

"IT'S A NOTE FROM OUR MASCOT....
HE'S HOLDING OUT FOR ONE HUNDRED GRAND!"

"THANKS, BUT I'LL PACK MY OWN LUNCH."

"ACE CAT FOOD COMPANY....WHAT'S THAT, SIR?..."

"IT'S ONE OF HIS EARLY ANCESTORS
WHO CHASED MICE FOR THE PIONEERS!"

© 1977
McNaught Synd., Inc.

CHOIR
PRACTICE
TODAY

" I'M VERY SORRY, BUT..."

"HE'D LIKE TO BORROW THE CAR TONIGHT."

"HEATHCLIFF!...GO HOME!"

"NICE TO SEE YOU, FRED...I'D BETTER GET BACK
AND FINISH THE MARQUEE."

"I HATE TO DISTURB YOUR AFTER-DINNER NAP, BUT...."

"HE'S PATROLLING IN AN UNMARKED CAR!"

© 1977
McNaught Synd., Inc.

© 1977
McNaught Synd., Inc.

"ALL YOU BUMS!...OUTA THE PARK!!"

"YEAH!...YOU TOO!"

"BUT THE DENTED CAT FOOD CANS ARE ON SALE, DEAR!"

"HE'S BEEN VOTED GRAND EXALTED RULER
OF THE LOYAL ORDER OF ALLEY CATS!"

"HAH!...MY KITE'S HIGHER THAN YOURS!"

"TONIGHT, IT'S A HOOTENANNY!"

"LET ME EXPLAIN.....THIS IS NOT THE ORIGINAL ARK..."

"HE'S MADE A POSITIVE IDENTIFICATION
FROM THE MUG SHOTS!"

"YOU'LL HAVE TO REMOVE YOUR T-SHIRT."

"AH!...I'M JUST IN THE MOOD FOR A MIDNIGHT SNACK!"

"HAVE YOU BEEN AT
THAT FISH TANK?!"

"WHO'S THE NEW GUY?"

"SORRY, SPIKE, BUT THE PASSWORD IS 'MEOW'!"

"HE DOESN'T LIKE IT WHEN I STAND AROUND
AND GOSSIP."

"LET ME EXPLAIN THE MASCOT'S JOB...."

"THERE'S SOMEONE HERE ABOUT OUR CAT FOOD!"

"YOU'RE NO RAY OF SUNSHINE ON A MONDAY MORNING!"

"HAVE YOU SEEN A FOX, LITTLE GIRL?"

"WHAT ABOUT THIS $700 IN YOUR MATTRESS?!"

"HAVE DECIDED NOT TO TAKE PRISONERS !"

© 1977
McNaught
Syndicate, Inc.

"WE NEVER SHOULD HAVE ASKED HIM TO PLAY 'GO FISH'!"

"NOTICE, MADAM, HOW NICELY IT PICKS UP THOSE DISGUSTING CAT HAIRS!"

"HE'S VERY SENSITIVE."

"HEATHCLIFF BELIEVES IN A BIG ENTRANCE!"

"LET'S YOU AND I HAVE A LITTLE TALK..."

"NO, NO,
HEATHCLIFF!"

"G'WAN!...IT
LOOKS YUMMY!"

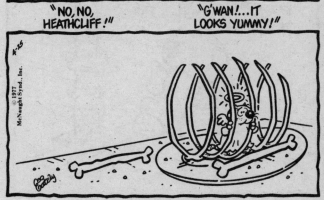

"WAIT 'TIL YOU SEE WHAT HE'S DONE WITH HIS SCRATCHING POST!"

"LOOK AT THIS MESS!...THAT CAT HAS DONE EVERYTHING
BUT STEAL OUR TRUCK!"

"HE'S RUNNING OFF WITH THE GYPSIES!"

"IT'S CLEAN CHICKEN!...YOU DON'T HAVE TO WASH IT!"

"CRUNCH!"

"WHO ?...THE POLICE DEPT.!
...DON'T TELL ME YOU'RE
AFTER HEATHCLIFF AGAIN!"

"NO...THIS TIME
IT'S SCOTLAND YARD!"

"THERE *WAS* A HOT DOG IN IT WHEN I PASSED IT DOWN THE AISLE!"

"I THINK HE GOT A WHIPLASH!"

© 1977
5-6 McNaught Synd., Inc.

"REMEMBER, GENTLEMEN, OUR SENSATIONAL NEW CAT FOOD FORMULA MUST BE KEPT IN UTMOST SECRECY!"

"...AND THE VILLAGERS WORSHIPED THE GREAT STONE IDOL..."

"WHAT HAPPENED, SMOKEY?"

"HE SIGNED ON FOR A HITCH WITH THE TUNA FLEET!"

"DID YOU TRY A WHITE FLAG OF SURRENDER?"

"BENEATH HIS ROUGH EXTERIOR,
BEATS A HEART OF GOLD!"

"RESPONSIBLE OPPOSING VIEWS TO THIS EDITORIAL
WILL BE GRANTED EQUAL TIME TO REPLY..."

"EEYAH!!"

"WHERE'S OUR POLAR BEAR RUG?"

"HE'S PERFECTED A BREED OF LARGE, ROASTER PARAKEETS!"

"HE'S GOING TO WEAR OUT THAT COPY OF 'MOBY DICK'!"

"STOP!-THIEF!!"

"THIS IS GETTING SERIOUS!"

"OH, OH!...HE'S IN ONE OF HIS PLAYFUL MOODS!"

"PLASTIC CANS DON'T MAKE ENOUGH NOISE TO SUIT HIM!"

"LOOK!...THERE ARE *FOUR* OF US GOING ON THIS TRIP!"

"MY TEETH !...I CAN'T FIND MY TEETH !"

"HEATHCLIFF WON 'BEST SMILE IN SHOW'!"

"DON'T MAKE SUCH A BIG DEAL OUT OF A LOST GOLF BALL!"

"WHAT'S HE DOING AT THE HEAD OF THE PARADE ?!!"

"YES...?"

"STRIKE THREE!...YOU'RE OUT!"

"WHO'D LIKE TO GO TO THE ANTIQUE CAR SHOW?!"

"I HATE TO BREAK UP YOUR BEACH PARTY, BUT...."

"WELL, THEY'RE NOT GOING TO MAKE ME EAT CROW!"

"NOBODY IS GOING TO EAT CROW!"

"YOUR DAD NEVER VISITS FOR LONG."